Original title:
Life, Love, and the Unanswered

Copyright © 2025 Creative Arts Management OÜ
All rights reserved.

Author: Elliot Harrison
ISBN HARDBACK: 978-1-80566-246-4
ISBN PAPERBACK: 978-1-80566-541-0

Carved in Time's Embrace

In a world where socks go to hide,
We search for logic, but it won't abide.
Like puzzle pieces lost in the air,
We laugh at the chaos without a care.

Jellybeans dance in a silly parade,
While otters in tuxedos prepare for a raid.
We juggle our dreams like hungry clowns,
Unraveling giggles as the clock spins 'round.

Shadows of a Shared Life

Two monkeys debate while sipping on tea,
One says, "I'm smart, the other, not me!"
Their chatter echoes through the high trees,
As they ponder if squirrels really have knees.

In the kitchen, toothpaste meets the bread,
What's for dinner? A mystery instead.
We share our secrets with a wink and a grin,
Like socks in the dryer, we're all mixed within.

The Journey Through Unanswered Dreams

Our wishes are stuck in a traffic jam,
Like a party of turtles each taking a slam.
With wide-open eyes, we watch the world twirl,
Chasing confetti as it gives way to swirl.

Chasing the sunrise on roller skates,
We bumble and tumble, adjusting our fates.
In the carnival of thoughts, we throw all our darts,
And hope they stick true to our whimsical hearts.

Glimmers of Hope in a Distant Glade

In a meadow where daisies wear polka dots,
We contemplate fruitcake and the strangest of thoughts.
A squirrel with a hat reads the news with a frown,
As butterflies giggle and dance, twirl around.

Amidst patchwork clouds, we make silly plans,
Like crafting a boat made of mismatched cans.
In this glade of wonders, our minds take flight,
Crafting laughter and stories that shine ever bright.

Secrets Hidden in the Heart's Embrace

In whispers soft, the secrets dwell,
A sock misplaced, a story to tell.
With jest and chuckle, we hide the key,
To treasure chests of absurdity.

In shadows cast by curious glances,
We dance around in silly prances.
Behind closed doors, a giggle brews,
As secrets blend like mismatched shoes.

When Time Says Goodbye

A tick, a tock, then off you go,
Time waves its hand, putting on a show.
With fond farewell, it steals our tea,
And leaves behind a mystery.

We chase it down the ticking street,
With mismatched socks and dancing feet.
Yet moments linger, full of cheer,
As we laugh about the things we fear.

Yearning for What Was Never Said

A word unspoken, a missed chance,
Like a cat that missed its silly dance.
We ponder jokes we should have cracked,
Instead, we sit, and quietly act.

With timid hearts, we sip our brews,
Regretting puns we ought to use.
In silence dwell the clever lines,
Like kittens tangled in their vines.

Threads of Fate in a Woven Dream

In dreams we weave a playful thread,
With silly tangles upon our bed.
Life's oddities twist and twirl,
A comedy in a wishful whirl.

A stitch of fate, a glimpse so bright,
We chuckle at the tangled sight.
Yet through the laughter, hope is spun,
In knots of joy, we come undone.

Beneath the Surface of Our Dreams

Beneath the waves of sleep we dive,
Chasing fish that sing and jive.
Napping on clouds, oh what a scene,
Where flying cats know where we've been.

Jumping through hoops made of dough,
With sprinkles that dance and glow.
In a land of socks and mismatched shoes,
We giggle at all the silly clues.

When Stars Collide in Silent Harmony.

When bright dots crash with a gentle thud,
A cosmic ballet, more magical than mud.
Galaxies spin in a wondrous waltz,
While comets draw mustaches—oh, what faults!

Under the watch of a smirking moon,
Planets play hopscotch, a comical tune.
With cosmic ice cream and sprinkles of light,
They celebrate mischief all through the night.

Eternity in a Glimpse

In a snapshot taken with no fuss,
Moments freeze like a bus in a rush.
We catch a glimpse of a cat in a hat,
Who's reading the news while chasing a rat.

Time trickles down like melted cheese,
Every droplet tickles, oh, such a tease.
The future tastes like a rainbow of fun,
As we dance in the sun until day is done.

Whispers of the Untold

In the corners where secrets swirl and spin,
Whispers tickle chins with a sly little grin.
A parrot tells tales of a dancing frog,
Who moonwalks through puddles, all covered in fog.

Bubbles of laughter burst in the air,
As jellybeans argue who's more rare.
In riddles of giggles, we skip and cheer,
Finding joy in the chatter, loud and clear.

Questions Linger in the Silence

Why do socks always go missing?
Is the dryer a sock-eating beast?
Did the cat plot a daring heist?
Or is it just laundry's cruel feast?

Do ducks ever quack in confusion?
Is that why they waddle with flair?
Is the pond a riddle unsolved?
Or just water without a care?

When you trip over air with a flail,
Does the ground conspire with the sky?
Is there a committee of clouds,
Deciding if you should fly or cry?

Can spaghetti really be a noodle?
Or is it a twist of fate on a plate?
Was there pasta that dreamed of being long,
And now it just dances on fate?

Heartbeats in the Quiet Hours

At midnight, my stomach rumbles bright,
Is it hungry, or just lonely at night?
Do cookies come alive when I sleep,
To hold parties and secrets to keep?

Why do we ponder absurd little things,
Like why do birds whistle and sing?
Do they know the secrets of the moon,
Or do they just think it's a big balloon?

If I text a shadow, will it reply,
Or just flicker away like a mischievous spy?
Can whispers of stars twinkle and blend,
Into messages only the dreamers comprehend?

In moments of silence, a laugh will burst,
From awkward thoughts that bubble and thirst.
Are we all just jesters in life's silly show,
Trying to pin down what we don't even know?

Unwritten Letters to the Stars

Dear stars, do you ever feel ungrounded?
Do you notice the dust we all strounded?
When the moon wears a grin with pride,
Is it laughing at the silly things we hide?

What do you do when you've lost your way?
Do you twinkle to guide or just sway?
When comets race by with flair and zest,
Are they chasing dreams or just taking a rest?

Why does the sun insist on waking me up,
With rays that spill like an overflowing cup?
Is it trying to share some bright, wild tale,
Or just ensuring I can't ever be stale?

If I wish on a star with all of my might,
Will it come true, or just giggle at night?
Maybe stars just chuckle at our requests,
And send back love as their cosmic jest!

The Dance of Fleeting Moments

Time tickles with a mischievous grin,
As moments slide slippery like skin.
Do butterflies giggle at our quick haste,
Or remind us to savor, not just to taste?

When I dance in my kitchen to old tunes,
Is the fridge my partner, or the brooms?
As I trip on a toe, with a laugh and a twirl,
Do the dishes roll their eyes, thinking it's cruel?

Why do we rush to the end of our days,
Chasing the clock in a dizzying blaze?
As if seconds could vanish if we hold tight,
But giggles come easier when we let go light.

If moments are fleeting, let's dance with the breeze,
And chase butterflies with the greatest of ease.
For in every chuckle and mishap that's spun,
Are the threads of our madness, stitched up for fun!

In the Embrace of the Unseen

Underneath the moonlit glow,
Llamas wear sunglasses for show.
Spinning tales with silly grace,
Kittens dance in outer space.

We chase dreams with rubber bands,
Building castles made of sand.
Who knew clouds could taste like pie?
Even ducks wear bowties, oh my!

Invisible friends throw a bash,
Wearing socks and bright green trash.
Whispers dance like fluttering leaves,
Expectations dressed in silly sleeves.

The clock laughs, it's time to play,
Inventing games as we drift away.
In the chaos, joy finds its place,
In the embrace of this unseen space.

A Palette of Mixed Emotions

Colors spill from a painter's brush,
Red squirrels join the wild rush.
A yellow sun wearing a frown,
While pink clouds float upside down.

A bluebird sings with a cheeky grin,
While rainbows wear shoes made of tin.
Joyful hiccups in an empty room,
As shadows dance with a twist of bloom.

With every giggle, sorrow sneaks,
A chocolate cake with salty peaks.
Dancing through a silly parade,
All feelings blend in a jumbled charade.

In this palette, laughter collides,
As sweet pickles rule the tides.
From blurry hearts that spin and swirl,
A tapestry of a wobbly world.

Flickers of Light in the Gloom

In the corners where dust bunnies play,
A glowworm leads the lost astray.
Jellybeans fall from heavens above,
Casting brightness like beams of love.

Hiccups echo through the dark,
While pet goldfish strut and spark.
A disco ball spins in a cupboard,
Fish dance wildly, dreams uncovered.

Lost socks whisper secrets to chairs,
Of sunny days and carefree flares.
Laughter echoes from the deep,
As shadows sneak in for a peep.

In this gloom, a wink and spin,
Every mishap turns to win.
With tickles in the darkest night,
Flickers of joy give hope a bite.

The Pathway of Uncharted Hearts

Stumbling down a winding lane,
Where jellybeans burst like rain.
Caterpillars wear tiny hats,
As wisdom's found in silly chats.

A zigzag path of marshmallow dreams,
Squirrels debate the best ice creams.
With every step, a giggle pops,
As wobbly tunes burst like soda shops.

Sidewalks giggle beneath our feet,
Where dancing shadows form a fleet.
In this world of dippy schemes,
Every heart composes its dreams.

We navigate with joyful art,
Creating maps with our quirky heart.
In this journey, strange but true,
The strangest paths lead me to you.

Footprints on the Edge of Time

Each tick of the clock shares a secret dance,
With mismatched socks in a comical glance.
We trip on the past like it's a silly prank,
As we giggle and wave from the glory bank.

Every wrinkle tells tales of cake and cheer,
Forgotten why we're here, yet we persevere.
Balancing spoons on our noses with flair,
Moments like these float in the open air.

We chase after dreams that refuse to sit still,
While the puppy in socks makes a mess on the grill.
Our footprints get tangled in gooey delight,
As laughter echoes through the heart of the night.

So here's to the blunders, the stumbles, the fun,
In this goofy parade, we're never outdone.
With footprints like jelly and giggles as rhyme,
We waddle together on the edge of time.

The Bridge Between Dreams and Reality

On a bridge made of marshmallows, we float and sway,
With candy canes painted in bright shades of gray.
The dreamers are juggling while sipping on tea,
And penguins tap dance, oh what sights to see.

Reality winks with a mischievous grin,
As we ride on the backs of a flock of finch kin.
We laugh at the clouds, they're just fluff on the scene,
Twirling beneath the wobbly moonlight sheen.

I asked the horizon, 'What's next on the map?'
He chuckled and said, 'It's all just a trap!'
We whirl through the wonders like it's part of the game,
In this bridge of our dreams, nothing's quite the same.

With a flick of a wand, we make wishes and cheer,
For the moments we capture that often disappear.
So let's skip through the meadows of nonsense and glee,
For reality is what we choose it to be!

Fragments of a Broken Song

A melody spins in the corner of time,
With hiccuping notes in a wacky rhyme.
We whistle along, though we're off-key for sure,
With laughter as lyrics that feel like a cure.

The piano plays hide-and-seek in the night,
While cats in top hats dance in fractured light.
Each verse is a puzzle, we stumble and fall,
As we giggle at friends who can't recall it all.

I find half a chorus stuck under a chair,
While our thoughts in a blender swirl round with great flair.
Tunes tumble like socks from a mischievous wash,
In a jangle of joy, we just laugh and posh.

Though fragments may scatter like leaves in the breeze,
We'll hum along giddily, do just as we please.
For each broken note is a chance to create,
A symphony silly that we celebrate!

Unraveled Threads of Connection

With yarn in our hands, we weave tales so bright,
While the cat's in the middle, plotting her slight.
We tangle our stories like spaghetti at noon,
With laughter unwinding beneath a full moon.

Connecting the dots with a wink and a nudge,
While the toaster demands we give it some fudge.
Each thread tells a joke, a twist in the tale,
As we ride on our bikes with one shoe and no mail.

A quilt of our moments hangs crooked and bold,
As mothers and fathers share secrets retold.
The fabric of friendship is stitched with a grin,
In this patchwork of chaos, we're happy to win.

So let's drop the stitches and laugh as we play,
As the threads of our days unravel and sway.
For in tangled connections, there's joy to be found,
And hugs made of laughter are what keep us bound.

The Echo of a Gentle Touch

In the quiet of the night,
A tickle brought to flight.
My heart skipped, took a leap,
Chasing giggles, not too deep.

Unexpected, quite absurd,
A whisper that felt unheard.
Caught in laughter, lost in jest,
Guess tomorrow's a new quest.

Yet, a sparkle in your eye,
Hints at secrets, oh my my!
Fingers dance on edges fine,
Do you see the joke is mine?

So we tumble through the dark,
Silly in our playful spark.
With each stumble, every fall,
We find joy in it all.

In the Twilight of Uncertainty

When the sun dips, shadows play,
Thoughts like cats begin to stray.
A quirk of fate, a silly glance,
Why did we do the awkward dance?

Eyes like searchlights, scanning bright,
Do we dare venture into the night?
With every wink and secret sigh,
We ponder if we're awfully shy.

In this haze, no plans in sight,
Just jokes that take off in flight.
We chuckle at the cosmic joke,
While tripping over dreams we stoke.

And when the dawn begins to crack,
We find the courage to look back.
Those moments tangled, wrapped in glee,
Are the puzzles, just you and me.

The Book of Forgotten Encounters

In dusty shelves, stories hide,
Of mishaps, laughs, and love's wild ride.
A spilled drink, a clumsy cheer,
Every chapter sheds a tear.

Pages turn with silly tunes,
As we dance beneath the moons.
With every blunder, sparks ignite,
Confessions made in pure delight.

Characters drawn with quirky flair,
Lifetime's lessons hanging bare.
Yet close the book, it's time to go,
But we giggle at what we know.

In tomorrow's unwritten tale,
We'll find laughter, hearts will sail.
Pages may close, but we'll recall,
The joy and folly that enthrall.

Resonance of a Thousand Moods

In the crowd, a silent cheer,
Electric vibes buzz all near.
Like jellybeans tossed in flight,
We blend colors, day and night.

A smile cracks, the tension breaks,
With every jest, a chance it makes.
Through pit stops and wild goose chases,
We find solace in funny faces.

The puzzles of hearts and minds,
Tickle toes, the joy it finds.
Shake the worries, let them stew,
As we stumble, me and you.

So here's to moods that bend and sway,
To foolish hope that leads the way.
With laughter echoing through our days,
We'll watch the world in silly ways.

Shadows Cast by Distant Flames

In a room full of whispers, jokes collide,
Where laughter hangs out like an uninvited bride.
The shadows hold stories of awkward friends,
Comedic misfortunes that never quite end.

The pizza delivery missed, oh what a feat,
We gathered our pennies to order some meat.
But in our own world, we dined with delight,
On invisible dishes and laughter's sweet bite.

The clock hands do tango in their own waltz,
While we tumble through memories, pulling our faults.
Each giggle's a treasure, each snort a gold mine,
In the sitcom of moments we label divine.

So here's to the moments, both silly and grand,
To shadows that flicker and dance hand in hand.
With smiles like fireworks lighting the air,
We cherish the laughter, the joy that we share.

Portraits of Gentle Heartbreak

With coffee cups clinking, we sketch our own fates,
Each sip filled with stories that twist and that wait.
Hearts in their pajamas, just watching TV,
While hope takes a nap on the softest of fleece.

We talk about pranks and the last slice of pie,
While glancing at photos of why and of why.
Each face tells a tale of affection gone dry,
Yet we laugh at the echoes of heartfelt goodbye.

The cat in the window seems part of the crew,
Throwing sass at our dramas and mischief, it's true.
In paintings of maybes and 'what could have been',
We find the bright colors that spark joy within.

So raise up your mugs to the bittersweet blend,
Of moments and mishaps that surely won't end.
We toast to the awkward, the odd and the rare,
For every soft sigh brings us laughter to share.

The Tapestry of Unseen Journeys

In bustling bazaars of missed starts and laughs,
We weave silly stories like colorful crafts.
Navigating twists where our compass spins,
Each step a new question, let the fun begin.

With hats made of wonder and shoes laced with glee,
We question the road that was never meant to be.
Map-less and reckless, we wander in style,
Poking at secrets, unraveling a smile.

From gardens of "maybe" to "oops, what a mess,"
We gather up treasures, our hearts in excess.
Each pitfall a party, each stumble a game,
As stories collect like a wild, funny frame.

So let's dance through the chaos, pretend we know more,
With wild goose chases that open the door.
For each twist of the tale adds a splash of surprise,
The journey is richer with laughter as prize.

A Path Not Taken and Its Ghosts

In the alleys of 'what ifs' we happily stray,
Ghosts of our choices like clowns come to play.
We chat with the shadows of paths left behind,
Where echoes of laughter leave memories blind.

Every door left unopened holds stories unspun,
Yet our hearts are like luggage, too heavy for fun.
With ghostly companions, we waltz down the hall,
Sipping on moments like sweet nectar's call.

Each fork in the road got a quirky embrace,
While we giggle at life's little unpredictable race.
With thumbs on the map and smiles dimming doubt,
We cherish the paths, even ones we're without.

So here's to the journeys we never quite took,
The fun-loving spirits that flourish in nooks.
With each silly choice, we dance and we sway,
For laughter's our compass, guiding the way.

Remnants of a Lost Embrace

In a café sat my heart, with a cake,
Sipping on dreams, too sweet to take.
A napkin's whisper, a fork's lament,
Hearts half-formed, a twisted event.

Balloons float by, in the morning sun,
Each one carrying tales of fun.
But where's the map to the missing sock?
I'll search the drawer, just around the clock.

Laughter's echo fills the air,
While I chase my shadow, unaware.
With crumbs of wishes upon my plate,
The tablecloth sighs, 'Oh, isn't fate great?'

In every sip, a story unsaid,
Like a cat who forgot how to tread.
Yet, I'll toast to the moments that tease,
With a wink and a dance, let's just appease.

Threads of Destiny's Fabric

A stitch in time, or was it a quilt?
Patterns of chaos, wrapped and built.
The sock drawer burst with the yarn of glee,
Knitting confusion for you and me.

Unraveled yarn on the living room floor,
Whispers of secrets we can't ignore.
There's a pom-pom party, what a sight!
With mismatched shoes, let's dance through the night.

The needle pricks where the laughter flows,
Each tug a giggle, such highs and lows.
Did we really think we'd sew it all right?
Oh, the joy in the messy delight.

Twiddling thumbs while the clock ticks by,
Beads of heroics that glitter and fly.
In the tapestry woven with threads of yore,
We find our heartstrings quietly roar.

In the Wake of Unanswered Questions

A chicken crossed the road with flair,
To ponder the 'why' of its daring affair.
With wings of doubt and toes of dread,
It asked the sky, 'What's up ahead?'

Between the clouds and the sunny beams,
Float snippets of half-formed dreams.
Why did I trip on that last banana peel?
Just life's little quirks wrapped up in a reel.

Questions hover like pesky flies,
Buzzing around with awkward sighs.
Do fish really know when they're out of water?
Or does the cat just try to be a plotter?

With a wink and a nod, we chase the mirage,
In search of giggles in the grand barrage.
Expecting answers like pizza on demand,
Yet finding joy in the unanswered strand.

Moonlit Reflections of a Soul

In the quiet glow of a silver night,
I tripped on thoughts, oh what a sight!
Stars twinkled gently, whispering dreams,
While I fumbled through life's puzzling schemes.

Shadows danced with a cheeky grin,
As I pondered where the stars had been.
Did I leave my keys in the galaxy's chair?
Or perhaps they're lost in a cosmic affair?

The moon chuckled, with beams of delight,
As I searched my pockets, oh so tight.
A reflection of laughter, a slip of fate,
Too busy to ponder, too challenged to wait.

Wanderlust hearts under starlit skies,
Spin tales of wonder as time gently flies.
With each little misstep, we hum a tune,
In the echo of night, beneath the wise moon.

Whispers in the Twilight

In the twilight, cats conspire,
Chasing shadows, hearts aspire.
With a giggle and a wink,
They plot more than we think.

Stars above wear silly hats,
Dancing nightly with the rats.
Crickets strum on guitar strings,
While fireflies share secret blings.

The moon grins with a silver grin,
It's the best time to begin.
With a tickle and a tease,
Every secret's sure to please.

So whisper with the cool night breeze,
Count your giggles, count your knees.
For in this twilight, laughs are free,
And every moment's a jubilee.

The Echo of Untold Stories

Echoes bounce on walls of time,
Silly tales in every rhyme.
A sock that vanished on its quest,
Now a legend, we can't rest.

Monkeys dressed in suits and ties,
Came to tea, oh what a surprise!
They sipped from cups and danced on floors,
While we cracked jokes and opened doors.

A snail forgot its way to home,
Wrote a book about how to roam.
Gave a lecture on the slide,
Unity, he claimed, was all inside.

So gather round for tales absurd,
Laughter is the sweetest word.
With stories swirling all around,
In this echo, joy is found.

Beyond the Veil of Dreams

In dreams where all the slippers fit,
Monkeys play a quirky bit.
Dancing stars in polka dots,
And ice cream melting in hot spots.

Whispers of a jellybean,
Bouncing high like a trampoline.
They sing of secrets, fun and free,
While bubbles float up a big tree.

A cat wears glasses, reading keen,
Stories of the in-between.
A hedgehog paints with vibrant hues,
While chameleons change their views.

So wander through this dreamer's place,
Like a wild, unstoppable race.
Wit and whimsy in every gleam,
Dive with joy into the dream.

Passion's Shadow on an Empty Canvas

On a canvas, shadows play,
Colorful thoughts chase the gray.
With every brush, a tickle's found,
As laughter echoes all around.

A squirrel dons a painter's hat,
Mixing colors, how about that?
While ants march to a rhythmic beat,
Bringing snacks for a delicious treat.

Splashes of joy, bright and bold,
A masterpiece beyond the mold.
With each stroke, more giggles grow,
A canvas where the wild things show.

So throw your worries to the wind,
Join the party that won't rescind.
In passion's shadow, join the fun,
For laughter's dance has just begun.

Echoes of What Should Have Been

In a world of socks unmatched,
I ponder if my fate's attached.
With every quirk that brings me cheer,
I laugh at what I hold so dear.

The coffee spills, the toast burns bright,
My plans go awry, but what a sight!
In quirky times, confusion gleams,
As I fumble through my wildest dreams.

The dance of chaos, a comical show,
Where I jump at every shadow I know.
Oh, the paths my mind has strayed,
Turned right, but left—what a charade!

Yet through the mess, I can't forget,
The joy in snafus that life begets.
So here's to the blunders, the slips, the fun,
For in these moments, we're all just one.

Unwritten Pages of Tomorrow

Today I scribble with no plan,
Drawing stick figures, just like a fan.
A to-do list that never ends,
With wishes written, and time bends.

I wonder about the plots I steer,
Will I become an astronaut, a deer?
With half a mind, I float away,
To lands of quests where goats can play.

The clock ticks on, my pen it crawls,
As if it holds the ancient calls.
But every doodle is part of the game,
A hodgepodge of dreams I can't quite name.

So here's to tomorrow, blank as can be,
A canvas wide for all to see.
When humor dances on every page,
It turns my quest into a stage.

The Veil of Unseen Paths

Behind the curtain, secrets hide,
In tangled woods, I take a ride.
With GPS that leads me wrong,
I stroll through paths where I don't belong.

A raccoon contests my sandwich prize,
While squirrels plot to claim the skies.
In every twist, the laughter flows,
As clumsiness becomes my prose.

Who knew the journey would bring such light?
With every stumble, I take flight.
A detour here, a laugh-filled fumble,
Turns every fall into a jumble.

So veil the wisdom, sprinkle the cheer,
Embrace the foolishness, have no fear.
For in the paths that twist and bend,
We find the stories that never end.

Tides of Unspoken Words

The waves crash loud, while whispers stay,
In silent thoughts, I lose my way.
With every glance that says too much,
I fumble feelings, oh, such a touch!

The fish don't care what I might say,
They swim along, come what may.
Each bubble floats, a thought unshared,
Where secrets linger, feeling bare.

Yet laughter tumbles like rolling foam,
Turning every quiet into a home.
With every wave, unvoiced and free,
I relish the mystery that comes to be.

So let's raise a toast to words unsaid,
To thoughts that dance just overhead.
In tides of echoes, our hearts may twirl,
In comic fashion, around the swirl.

Drifting on the Winds of Tomorrow

A kite, a cat, a burrito in flight,
Chasing after dreams, with all of our might.
A sock on the floor, it's playing the fool,
While we dance with the breeze, like it's just a cool school.

Laughter erupts as we stumble and trip,
Falling through joy, on a comical slip.
Chasing the sunset in mismatched shoes,
With popcorn-filled pockets and endless good news.

A fortune cookie promise that says we'll be great,
But we still can't remember our last dinner date.
With each quirky twist, our fates intertwine,
Sipping on lemonade, we toast to our shine.

So drift through the chaos, let whimsy take hold,
For stories unfold in colors so bold.
Embrace all the blunders, they're part of the game,
In this wild ride together, we'll never be the same.

A Realm Where Questions Linger

Do penguins really wear tuxedos at night?
Why do we think socks can't pair up just right?
Are tacos just dreams wrapped in a shell?
In this whimsical world, who really can tell?

Why don't cows ever start a band on the grass?
Is the moon made of cheese or just humor amassed?
With giggles and theories, we ponder and play,
In the realm of the curious, we skip through the day.

Did you ever wonder where missing things go?
Like that one left shoe, or your favorite show?
In a land full of chuckles, we chase after fun,
And celebrate questions, for there's always more to run.

So let's build a castle of whimsy and smiles,
With a moat of deep laughter stretching for miles.
In this enchanted place, where wonders all sing,
We'll dance through the questions that joy often brings.

Celestial Echoes of Our Yearnings

Stars playing hide and seek in the night,
With giggles that echo, such a curious sight.
Do they laugh when we trip over our shoes?
Or ponder our snacks, like they're evening news?

A comet whizzes by, wearing a hat,
It shouts, "Hey, don't sweat it! Just look where you're at!"

With our hearts all aglow in this cosmic spree,
We toast to the wishes—the misses—we see.

Alien whispers float on the breeze,
"Ask us your secrets, we'll do as you please!"
In the labyrinth of stars, we juggle our dreams,
Spinning tales of laughter, or so it seems.

A dance with the cosmos, inflatable and bright,
With the wobble of planets, we drift through the light.
So let's reach for the stars, or just reach for a snack,
In this celestial giggle, there's always room to crack.

The Melody of Untold Stories

A banjo strums gently under a tree,
With squirrels as the backup, just wait and see.
Each twang a reminder of moments so grand,
When we laughed till we cried—oh, wasn't it planned?

In the library of echoes, tales blur and blend,
Where the cat is the hero, and time can just bend.
With secrets a'whisper and mischief afoot,
Scribbled in margins, where shenanigans hoot.

A pizza delivery, but no one's at home,
The cheese winks and giggles; it starts to roam.
With each slice a chapter, we savor the crust,
In pies of enchantment, we dance with our trust.

So gather 'round closely, let's spin yarns anew,
Chasing raccoons in tuxedos, it's true!
With melodies bubbling from laughter-filled hearts,
In this world of adventure, the fun never departs.

Cracked Mirrors and Shattered Reflections

Once I saw my face today,
It looked a little hazy,
With a grin that said, "Hello!"
And hair that looked so crazy.

I laughed at all the cracks,
Each one tells a story,
Of failed attempts at dance,
And the search for lost glory.

The mirror said, 'Try again,'
With a wink and a gleam,
So I strutted down the hall,
Living out my wildest dream.

But the floor is still a trap,
I stumbled on a shoe,
The mirror just cracked up,
As if it already knew.

Serenades of an Untouched Soul

If my heart could sing a tune,
It would hum like a fridge,
A little off-key and loud,
Like a cat on a bridge.

I serenade the empty room,
With socks piled high in stacks,
It echoes back a lonely tune,
But hey, at least it claps!

My coffee cup joins in the cheer,
Spilling notes on my lap,
Yet here I sit and ponder,
While the world takes a nap.

And though I may be untouched,
By romance, cool and bold,
I'll dance with my reflections,
In rhymes—unbought and sold.

The Weight of a Thousand Goodbyes

With every wave I threw,
I felt a suitcase grow,
Full of all my reckless dreams,
And last-minute shows.

Goodbyes are such a weight,
Like rocks in my shoe,
I trip through all the memories,
Some old, but mostly new.

I packed my favorite snacks,
For a flight I never take,
Instead, I sit and munch away,
On all the paths I make.

Yet still, I wave goodbye,
To times I wish to keep,
Just me and my suitcase,
And a promise not to weep.

Silent Conversations with the Moon

Underneath the silver glow,
I chat with that round face,
It chuckles at my deep thoughts,
While I search for my place.

I ask it all my questions,
About stars and their flights,
But it just beams back at me,
In the still of the nights.

We swap secrets and giggles,
As crickets chirp their song,
But the moon just winks at me,
Saying, 'You're where you belong.'

In this cosmic banter,
With a friend so far away,
I find my thoughts are endless,
As I laugh at yesterday.

When Time Stands Still

In moments where the clock's a fool,
We laugh as we float in a timeless pool.
Minutes blend like ice cream swirls,
Tick-tock dances, hilarious whirls.

A squirrel insists it's noon by his watch,
While my cat claims she's on a much longer stretch.
Time giggles as it prances away,
We sip on moments like fine cabernet.

Pajamas become our daily attire,
And chores transform into a comedy choir.
With socks on our hands and pots on heads,
We banter about books that we never read.

So here we sit, with laughter our guide,
Where seconds and hours take a silly slide.
In this pause where nothing's amiss,
We find the joy in the time that we kiss.

The Unwritten Love Letters

In drawers they hide, penned phrases ignored,
Promises of lunch that were happily stored.
Yet paperclips rust in a dusty embrace,
While coffee spills humor on misshapen grace.

To write of my heart would take more than ink,
For you make me ponder - oh, what do you think?
But thoughts tumble out like mismatched socks,
In the chaos of feelings, I lose track of clocks.

Cupid's arrows got caught in a glitch,
His letters unread, he's found in a ditch.
So with giggles we pen such a jumbled affair,
Ink spills like secrets we're too shy to share.

Yet in these lost pages, the laughter takes flight,
Words of affection all wrapped up in light.
For though not a letter will ever get sent,
The joy of your smile is my love's true intent.

Riddles of the Heart's Compass

With a compass that's spinning, we laugh at the map,
Leading us to corners where we both took a nap.
What's north when the south feels like marshmallow fluff?
In riddles we whirl like two leaves in a bluff.

Your grin points the way, though none planned this route,
As we tumble through life, amid giggles and doubt.
X marks the spot where the kitchen was said,
But I found the ice cream tucked under the bed.

Mismatched directions only fuel the fun,
For every lost turn brings us closer, hon.
A treasure of laughter in all that we do,
As our hearts weave the tales that are perfectly blue.

So let's roam these riddles with joyful delight,
Through paths of confusion that end in the night.
With compass in hand, we'll solve every pose,
For the bliss found in laughter forever grows.

Unmapped Journeys of Togetherness

Two wanderers lost in the whimsical charts,
Explore galaxies spun with their spinning hearts.
Maps are redundant when you have a smile,
And absurdity stretches their journey for miles.

In clouds made of cupcakes, we drift through the skies,
Where rain from above is just fizzy surprise.
With each step we take, we trip on our dreams,
And build castles of taffy with eccentric schemes.

Every detour we find is a chance for some fun,
Where the bluebirds hold dances when day's finally done.

Through unmarked paths, we'll stumble and grin,
For the sweetest of travels, oh, they all begin!

So here's to the journey, with warmth in our souls,
Chasing the sunshine, unearthing the shoals.
For every wrong turn is just a new way,
To find joy in the madness - come laugh, let's play!

Chasing Stars Across a Distant Sky

Between the clouds, we float and twirl,
With cosmic dreams that dance and swirl.
We throw a wish on a shooting star,
Only to find it's an old candy bar.

Galaxies spin in a wobbly way,
We chase them down, or forget to pay.
Astronauts giggle in zero-gravity bliss,
While filling vacuum bags with cosmic mist.

Yet still we leap, heads full of grand schemes,
For what is life but a series of dreams?
A telescope shows us the world from afar,
But all we see is a fast food jar.

So launch your hearts to the vibrant night,
And don't forget to hold on tight.
For in this chase, remember this line,
Even in space, you'll still need to dine.

The Color of Longing

I painted wishes in shades of green,
Hoping they'd sprout, if you know what I mean.
But they turned out blue, just like my mood,
If longing was art, I'd be widely viewed.

In a garden of thoughts, I plant seeds of desire,
Water them gently, and watch them expire.
But if hope were a flower, I'd have a bouquet,
That wilts in the sun; guess I'll try shade today.

The canvas is messy with dreams gone awry,
Brushstrokes of laughter, a heartfelt goodbye.
Still, I tomfool and shuffle, with paint on my face,
A Jackson Pollock of glorious disgrace.

So come take a stroll through this colorful mess,
And let's chuckle together at this grand "success."
For every hue speaks of a tale left to tell,
In shades of our wishes, we puzzle quite well.

Beneath the Surface of Tomorrow

Tomorrow whispers with a cheeky grin,
Like a puppy who thinks it will surely win.
It struts around like it's got something cool,
While I trip over plans, like a frazzled fool.

Underneath the bed, hope often resides,
Next to the dust bunnies that clutter our strides.
We make grand designs of what's yet to come,
But usually end up with popcorn and gum.

The calendar mocks with its neatly drawn lines,
Yet I'm busy dodging my own deadlines.
A treasure map leads to a pitiful stew,
While tomorrow just giggles, like, "What's up with you?"

So lay down your worries, let chaos unfold,
For who really knows what tomorrow will hold?
With each tick of the clock, let's toast with a cheer,
To the funny old nonsense we hold very dear.

Remnants of a Forgotten Promise

In the attic of memories, dust bunnies roam,
Where promises linger, like stray socks from home.
I vowed to be dignified, wise, and sincere,
But here I am giggling, with a cupcake in cheer.

Old plans lay scattered, like toys on the floor,
A jigsaw of hope that we never explore.
I swore I'd write poems with elegance and flair,
Yet here I am rhyming about napping in a chair.

The echoes of vows ring out with a laugh,
As I trip over dreams on my self-made path.
Each "maybe tomorrow" comes rushing to play,
But who really wants to work on a day?

So raise a glass to the broken decree,
For all of its flaws, it's still part of me.
With humor and giggles, let's celebrate fate,
And rejoice in the chaos—aren't we first-rate?

Echoes of What Remains Unspoken

Beneath the laughter, there's a sigh,
A joke misplaced, we now know why.
With every wink, confusion grows,
Like trying to smell a blooming rose.

We dance on tracks of tangled fate,
While missing trains that run too late.
A text unsent that haunts the night,
Like ghosts that share their favorite fright.

We juggle thoughts like spinning plates,
Yet drop one loud in awkward states.
The punchline hides, it plays real coy,
Still seeking joy, oh silly ploy!

In conversations kept at bay,
We giggle softly, words atplay.
Each chuckle lingers, fingertips
On sentences lost through silly slips.

The Garden of Faded Hopes

In a patch where daisies used to bloom,
Now weeds have claimed the greatest room.
A gnome with a grin, so out of date,
Stands guard at dreams that can't relate.

The veggies sprout like rumors do,
Green beans whisper, 'We once knew you!'
A carrot here, a pumpkin there,
Nods at wishes floating in the air.

With trowels that chase forgotten schemes,
We dig for laughs and lost extremes.
Each root we pull sparks fun debates,
About the carrots and their fates.

When nature's joke plays on our minds,
Sunflowers giggle, pollens unwind.
In this odd garden, we tend our dreams,
With humor stitched through all the seams.

A Symphony of Unseen Connections

In a concert hall where seats are bare,
The echoes dance like they've no care.
Violins play for a cat's delight,
As music notes take off in flight.

The maestro waves a frantic hand,
While squirrels drum to a hidden band.
A symphony for shadows cast,
In ridiculous tones, the moments last.

A trumpet's honk brings smiles and grins,
As pianos tinkle, laughter wins.
We clap for cats, the stars above,
With every note, we share a love.

Behind the scenes, the silence waits,
For whimsical tunes that dance as mates.
In every silence, there is a sound,
Of connections deep, absurdly profound.

In Search of the Twilight's Whisper

As twilight sprawls on evening's cheek,
A star winks back, oh so unique.
The crickets chirp their nighttime song,
While fireflies flash where we belong.

With lanterns lit, we stroll in glee,
Chasing whispers that cannot flee.
A glance exchanged, a shrug for fun,
In this twilight game, we've only begun.

The moon peeks out, pulls up a chair,
Joining our secrets, oh it's so rare.
Spinning tales with the breezy air,
With chuckles that drift just everywhere.

In shadows long, we find our play,
Embracing jokes both light and gray.
As night unfolds and laughter calls,
We chase the whispers until night falls.

Silhouettes of Unbroken Promises

In a world of hopeful daydreams,
Promises dance like shadowed beams.
They leap and twirl, yet often hide,
Leaving us guessing where they bide.

With whispered vows that float and sway,
They decline to show us the way.
Like flirting notes tossed on a breeze,
They giggle, teasing, just to tease.

Yet here we stand, with hearts on sleeves,
Chasing shadows through the leaves.
Maybe one day they'll choose to stay,
And teach us how to laugh and play.

But until then, let's raise a cheer,
To promises that linger near.
For every joke they play, we swear,
This dance of hopes is quite the affair!

Moments that Slip Through Fingers

Tiny seconds like grains of sand,
Escape our fingers, oh so bland.
We grasp for joy, for it to remain,
Yet find it lost in a comical chain.

Each tick of the clock's a cheeky tease,
A trickster playing hide-and-seek with ease.
We chase time down a winding lane,
And laugh when it leaps right back again.

Fleeting flickers, quick as a wink,
Slipping away faster than we think.
We clutch at moments, like jelly in hand,
Just to find it wiggles, slips, and stands.

In our hustle, we often find,
That chasing laughter's the grandest grind.
So let's toast to the seconds that flee,
With a chuckle and a nod—just you and me.

The Weight of Unshed Tears

They sit on the edge with a heavy pause,
Tears that dangle, defying laws.
Like mischievous children hiding behind a door,
Just waiting to spill, but wanting more.

Each droplet's got a story to tell,
Of awkward moments where we fell.
They hold their breath and steal the show,
As if the world should only know.

Giggles echo, but the tears remain,
A heavy heart wears a funny chain.
They pull us down yet lift us high,
A circus act with every sigh.

So when you see them creeping near,
Remember the jest and shed a cheer.
For in every tear that might just fall,
Is a giggle waiting to enthrall.

An Odyssey of Hidden Desires

Through secret whispers, we plot and scheme,
Our dreams float by like a comical meme.
They teeter on the edge of a sigh,
With eyes wide open, we ask 'Oh, why?'

Chasing wishes with the grace of a cat,
Falling over thoughts that go splat.
We paint our hopes in colors bright,
Only to trip in the dead of night.

In the corner of our little minds,
Lay hidden treasures that wait to find.
Yet often they sneer as we pretend,
To grasp at humor, till the very end.

So let's embark on that zany quest,
For elusive dreams that never rest.
With laughter as our guiding star,
Who knows just how silly dreams can spar?

Paradoxes of Connection

Two hearts dance but trip on toes,
Like shoes too big where laughter grows.
A glance that sparks with playful zest,
Yet leaves us guessing what is best.

We text with thumbs, but few reply,
With emojis that wink, then die.
A joke that lands yet falls so flat,
In the circus of where we're at.

Between the lines, we often stray,
With maps that lead us miles away.
Connections bloom like flowers bright,
Then fade at dawn, without a fight.

A riddle wrapped in every hug,
An electric touch, then a shrug.
Bittersweet is our foolish game,
Yet somehow, we're always the same.

The Language of Unsaid Goodbyes

We smile like fools in crowded rooms,
While silence hangs like heavy looms.
A wave that feels like it should say,
'Hello!' instead of 'Go away!'

The clock ticks loud, but we just stand,
With words unspoken, hearts outstretched hand.
A nod that echoes, a tear that gleams,
As laughter hides our broken dreams.

In whispers lost, a million vows,
Yet every promise starts to bow.
With each good night that never ends,
The quiet frays our funny bends.

Here's to the chaos of our hearts,
Where hints deliver their false arts.
In the game of wait, the punchline lies,
In every glance, the unsaid goodbyes.

A Tapestry of Silent Longings

Threads interweave in secret schemes,
Like tangled yarn in fading dreams.
With whispers soft as falling snow,
We stitch our hopes that no one knows.

Crafted smiles hide desires deep,
Each heartbeat's rhythm, ours to keep.
A tapestry of what we crave,
Yet we are too proud, too brave.

In the silence, our souls collide,
With glances that shimmer, then divide.
A riddle spun in our disguise,
With laughter that sometimes gives rise.

In these shadows, we dare to play,
With hearts that mimic night and day.
A fabric rich, yet threadbare too,
In this comedy of me and you.

The Heart's Labyrinth of Choices

A winding maze of quirky signs,
With twists and turns, and funky lines.
Each choice a jester, bold and bright,
With no clear path, yet pure delight.

A left, a right, we laugh and pause,
Like kids playing tag with silly laws.
With every step, a hilarious fate,
Who knew indecision could be great?

In this maze, we chase the absurd,
With punctured hearts and laughter stirred.
A paradox, our footsteps trace,
In this merry dance, we find our place.

Yet through the quirks, a truth shines clear,
That all the choices we hold dear,
Lead us in circles, bold and bright,
In the labyrinth lit by sheer delight.

When Wishes Meet Reality's Edge

I wished for wings, to fly so high,
But tripped on shoelaces, oh my, my!
A dream of clouds, I thought I'd see,
Instead, I sprawled on ground quite free.

I asked for riches, gold and charms,
But found a penny in my palms.
The universe laughed, took a break,
And said, 'A joke? Just for your sake!'

In stores of wishes, I browsed around,
Found laughter and joy for free, abound.
Yet here I stand, still wishing more,
With laundry piles, bursting galore!

So let's chuckle at dreams gone wild,
Like kids caught laughing, every child.
When wishes come true, they often twist,
In ways unexpected, but still, persist!

Reveries of What Might Have Been

I pondered paths that could have bloomed,
Yet here I sit, unkempt and doomed.
With every choice a fork in hand,
Who knew snack time would be so grand?

Imagined brilliance, a scholar's fate,
But here I am—oh, isn't it great?
With my degree in naps and snacks,
A scholar's twist on all my hacks.

I dreamed of travel, of far-off lands,
Yet Netflix called with open hands.
My passport's dusty, but what the heck,
The couch is comfy and worth the check!

So here's to dreams of what might be,
With giggles shared, just you and me.
We'll pop some popcorn, share absurd tales,
In cozy realms where no one fails!

The Unfolding Story of Us

Our tale began on a Tuesday night,
A spilled drink turned everything right.
You laughed so hard, the soda flew,
And I knew then, my heart just knew.

We danced like fools in the moonlit glow,
Two clumsy hearts moving too slow.
Your foot met mine in a joyful way,
"Our love's a trip—hip-hip-hooray!"

Stories spun from the chaos around,
Each plot twist a giggle shared, profound.
With epic fails and coffee grounds,
We wrote a book with silly sounds!

The pages turned with each blunder bold,
Every chapter more fun than told.
So here's to us, the quirky crew,
With laughter and whimsy in all we do!

Fables of Two Souls Entwined

Once upon in a land quite kooky,
Two souls met, oh, wasn't that spooky?
Together they laughed at the silliest things,
Like tripping on air and birdcage swings.

Their story wove through hiccups and sighs,
From burnt dinners to spontaneous pies.
With hearts intertwined like spaghetti strands,
They danced through chaos, hand in hand.

In jest they spoke of epic quests,
Like finding the best, the fluffiest vests.
Each adventure a chapter, each chuckle a page,
In the book of their friendship, oh, what a stage!

So here's to the tales of mishaps galore,
Where fun is the treasure, and laughter's the score.
Two souls united in whimsical zest,
Creating a fable—now that's the best!

When Stars Align and Drift

Stars above play hide and seek,
Planets wobble, cosmic peek.
Gravity's pull, a funny dance,
While comets giggle, spin, and prance.

Galaxies tease with their twinkling light,
Lost socks in the black of night.
Asteroids chase in a comical race,
While aliens laugh at our silly face.

Nebulas puff with a colorful flair,
While stardust floats through cosmic air.
Every blink, a mystery unfolds,
In a universe, so funny, so bold.

So here we twirl on this playful rock,
Bearing secrets in every tick of the clock.
As the stars align then drift away,
We chuckle along, come what may.

A Canvas of Unexpressed Thoughts

Brushstrokes whisper on the canvas wide,
Colorful giggles that we cannot hide.
Thoughts run wild, a splattered spree,
While sticky fingers mean a mess, you see.

Penguins waddle in hues of blue,
Jellybeans bring a vibrant hue.
Statements float like marshmallows high,
Yet no one knows just why they fly.

Palette of dreams in a hilarious twist,
Where shy wishes dance, never missed.
Each blank space holds a chuckle or two,
As the unspoken turns into a hue.

A canvas where silence has much to say,
With laughter's echo, we find our way.
For in the brush, there's a tale to share,
Of all the moments caught in mid-air.

The Silence Between Us

In the gaps where chuckles lie,
Noses crinkle, no need to try.
Words escape like squirrels on a spree,
While laughter hovers, light and free.

Muffins soften the awkward pause,
Critters scurry with comical cause.
A wink exchanged, a knowing grin,
As memories bubble, let the fun begin.

The air is rich with unspoken glee,
Like confetti floating, wild and free.
When silence reigns, it's not a crime,
Just a melody, playing in time.

Hidden jokes and glances say more,
Adding flavor like popcorn to a score.
Between us, mysteries chatter and tease,
In this stillness, we find our ease.

A Journey Through the Infinite

Riding rockets on a noodle trail,
Spinning wildly, we'll never fail.
Clouds of cotton candy delight,
Wishing stars dance in the night.

Skipping through realms where giggles thrive,
Chasing shadows, feeling alive.
Hopscotch on moons, oh what a sight,
With tickles of space dust, pure delight.

Sailing through laughter, we float on a beam,
In the twilight of moments, we dream a dream.
Cosmic clown cars zoom in a line,
Creating mischief, a natural sign.

So grab a buddy, hop on this ride,
The infinite await, with arms open wide.
In the journey of giggles, our spirits will lift,
As we bounce through the cosmos, a joyful gift.

Shadows of a Heart's Yearning

In a world where socks go missing,
And the cat thinks it's a king,
I ponder on my antics,
Like a quirky jester in spring.

The dinners I accidentally burn,
With smoke signals I send in mirth,
They say I'm culinary challenged,
But I'm a chef of laughter's worth.

Chasing dreams on roller skates,
With one wheel wobbling in flight,
I'm hoping for a graceful fall,
That turns into a comedy night.

Among the plants that I forget,
And the dust bunnies that I feed,
I discover truths in chaos,
And chuckle at how I mislead.

Fleeting Moments

A butterfly lands on my nose,
And for a minute, time blurs,
With giggles echoing like chimes,
Life's silly little detours.

The ice cream melts before I sip,
It dribbles down my favorite shirt,
But laughter masks the sticky mess,
As I pretend I'm wearing art.

In a race where I tripped on fate,
I laughed and rolled like a pro,
The finish line's a phantom here,
But I'll steal the show, don't you know?

Moments slip like soap in hands,
Slippery, yet full of charm,
And I dance with the absurdity,
In this sweet, chaotic balm.

Endless Echoes

I shout into the empty void,
A sock puppet greets my call,
In echoing, absurd responses,
Laughter rises, then we fall.

Trading texts with furry friends,
While they plot to steal my chair,
In a world of silly whispers,
My heart skips beats of playful air.

Chasing shadows on sunny streets,
With my thoughts doing a jig,
Every step a comedic sketch,
As life dances, tiny and big.

We stumble through this jolly mess,
With echoes that follow our tracks,
And in each chuckle, I'll find peace,
In the laughter that never lacks.

The Dance of Forgotten Dreams

I dream of tangoing with a chair,
In the moonlight's whimsical glow,
With every turn, I trip and spin,
My partner, a pot with a bow.

Instead of stars, I talk to lamps,
Convinced they hold the wisest tales,
As I twirl till the morning comes,
With laughter stuck in my sails.

My ambitions float like balloons,
In a gusty wind of despair,
Yet I laugh with their sudden pops,
They teach me not to beware.

In this circus of silly schemes,
Where dreams stumble like a clown,
I'll wear my heart like a funny hat,
And spin through my own upside down.

Between Heartbeats and Hesitation

I ponder on which shoes to wear,
As if it's really a grand affair,
While the world spins dizzy on choice,
I giggle at the nothing to compare.

Should I text or air my thoughts loud,
With emojis dancing in my mind?
Both options feel like riddles, dear,
Like trying to catch a cloud unkind.

The moments hang like cotton candy,
Sweet, yet fleeting like a thread,
I laugh at how absurd it gets,
Finding joy in what's left unsaid.

In this realm of quirky pauses,
With every heartbeat, a silly dance,
I embrace the silly little doubts,
For laughter's always worth a chance.

www.ingramcontent.com/pod-product-compliance
Lightning Source LLC
Chambersburg PA
CBHW071834160426
43209CB00003B/296